Journey OF A Maturation Rollercoaster

Written by

GREQUAN CARTER

Journey of a Maturation Rollercoaster
Copyright © 2018 by Grequan Carter

ISBN: 978-1-54393-739-8 (Print)
ISBN: 978-1-54393-740-4 (eBook)

Table of Contents

Vocabulary Reference

Throughout this book you may experience language you're unfamiliar with. I'm fully aware of words that are presented as misspelled. This reference page consist of words utilized throughout the book and their corresponding meaning.

Thot- refers to a woman that is easily persuaded to engage in sexual acts or voluntarily offers to do so with multiple individuals they just met or previously met. Or all of the above. (Guys can be identified in this term as well.)

Gunna- going to.

Gotta- got to.

Tryna- trying to.

Boutta- about to.

Cuz- because.

Sus- is acting suspicious or not right.

Imma- im going to.

Gon- going to.

Grilling- intense eye contact.

Lit- Being in an upbeat mood or something being cool or fun.

Facts- is a true statement or agreeing with something.

Dogma- a principle that you cannot deny that it is true.

Flexing- showing off or displaying personal gear, like clothes or a car.

Thee- you.

Subterfuge- deceit in order to achieve ones goal.

Lackin- not being on point, slacking, not paying attention, lack of awareness to any situation or not doing what you have to do to progress.

Bread- form of money.

Cop something- purchasing/buying something.

Popped off- a male performing sexual acts to a female or a crisis happening at the spur of the moment.

Popped on- aggressively attacking someone or getting aggressively attacked.

Kat(s)- refers to a person or multiple people.

Hit- a past tense word that means that you or someone had sexual intercourse with someone.

Debo- a character from the movie "Friday" who is the neighborhood bully, who happens to be cross eyed. He also got knocked out by another character named Craig.

Celow- a dice game that utilizes 3 dice.

Neck- is a blowjob.

Breeze- is to leave from somewhere.

Gear- is any type of clothing or accessory.

"I'm feeling you"- means I like you.

"Held it down"- looked out for someone in a good way. (Hold it down is the present tense.)

I wanted to start off by saying, the fact that you even have this book in your possession has made you worthy of me expressing my appreciation for you! Whether you love, like, hate or don't know me at all I still appreciate you! What motivated me to write this book are people like you. Everyone has their own uniqueness and I find that very intriguing. Especially if I had the opportunity to meet you, got to know you, or had an intimate moment with you. You're reading this book because you're meant to read it. Everything happens for a reason. Plus, you'll get exposure to a perspective I'm sure will relate to you in some way.

This book consist of me talking in a poetic voice throughout. Prepare yourself for a variety of voices, used to express different points. If you become puzzled, refer to the Vocabulary Reference page. This book requires you to think! To think and reflect upon yourself, and also the perspective of other individuals as well.

The goal is to help you look inside of yourself and find appreciation, courage, confidence, empathy, acceptance, inclusion and most importantly love! You may not experience all of the above, but if you absorb at least one, I'm SURE it'll help progress some aspect of your life. You deserve to experience happiness within your life. Reading this book and consciously absorbing the information will guide a closer path to your happiness.

Read pieces more than once! I want you to get the most from this book. Ask yourself, what does this mean? How does this relate to me? Now that I read that, what should I do? Depending on who you are, will determine how much action is taken. Just know action is required! Whether its word of mouth, writing something down or you physically doing something for yourself or another, something needs to be done. There is always room for growth in all of us. For example, when reading:

My brain brings brilliant bold thoughts about a beautiful blissful world but abandon by its people because nature is boring and broadcasting belligerent buffoons battling is better –G. Carter

What goes through your mind after reading that? What does that poem mean to you? Constantly think of those questions after reading a piece. Then read it again.

Throughout the book you will come across hands-on activities for you to participate in. I was a REC major in college so I'm all about having fun and playing games, and I want to share that with you. Plus the activities will help increase your pattern recognition ability, leading to you being able to put more meaning behind the pieces you'll read.

Enjoy!

Ball is Life

I ball so hard its abuse
I gun it from a left angle
Call me obtuse

My game on point
Like I'm A.I
So if you guard me too close bet imma go by

I rise up
Damn
Gre fly

Tryna jump with me I dare you to try
Get dunked on I'm Vince in his prime
Passes on Rondo I'm nice with the dimes

Tony Allen flow ill lock a nigga up
Cut to the hoop lob city going up
MJ era that's where I wanna be
Novak fever so you know I wet the three

Take the game over
Yea I'm so Kobe
MVP winner so you know I took the trophy

Bankshot I'm Duncan
Blake Griff I stay dunking
Call your girl LBJ cuz she constantly chocking

I'm hungry and hard working
My nickname should be Jokim
Niggas hating on me cuz their jump shot really broken
Watching on the side as my jump shot steady stroking
Coach he won't pass the ball
Don't worry he working

3-2-1
I hit the game winner
I only had 22 Tiago Splinter

I crossover he hit the ground
These wild bitches is on me now
They get low and they blow me down
I'm the hottest nigga in the town

–GreakaDisrespectful

Hoes Illusion

Got this Chinese bitch name Chi Lee
She flexible and freaky
I smack her ass while her butt in my face I'm calling her Rikishi

All my hoes give good neck
Anna Marie my fuck pet
Jackie Lisa Tonya Debra my splish-splash crew cuz they so wet

Me and my sons we taking over
Get high get lucky call it four leaf clover
Got hoes on deck and we bend them over
I blew Ivy so call me Hova

Got Ashley who like sex toys
That Woody Light-Years Bulls Eye
Got Tiffani who like bad boys
She diddy-bop I pop that's cream pie

Got Ronda and Rashawnda,
Got a thick black bitch from Rwanda
Got a hoe bitch
She a slow trick that take pride when she blow dick

When I see a MILF I take her down
Now she singing no Chris Brown
Imma big deal and I got bread so I call Tyra B for some 4 head

–GreakaDisrespectful

Succeed from Struggle

I'm living a life I know isn't for me. Oblivious to the eye, because I look kind of fly, but in reality I'm just hardly getting by. Bad bathroom, broken brooms, burnt bread and a bed hard as baboon that bruises my back is brutality! Filth frequently filling our living facility forcing false familiarities about how we function frustrates mom dukes. In order to progress, I will optimize myself with optimist and obviate obstacles. I will need an optimistic mentality. I'm educated and have the knowledge to succeed. But to grow I must have an idea and plant it as a seed.

-GC

Hood Antics

Late night walk from the park
Got stopped by the cops
They asked why you out so late?

Told em I was playing in the park
Just working on my moves
Going hard
I'm tryna be great.

Cop said did you see a kid with a black hoodie on
Pants low with a gun at the waist?

I said nope,
They looked at me like a joke,
And sped off like a fucking speed boat.

I walked straight
Then I made a right
Then I made a left
Walked straight then I saw my nigga Drew.

He pulled up
Hoodie up
Slow walk
Pants low
Eyes red and asked me what I'm boutta do?

I told him I'm about to eat good,
Got some mac and cheese
I eat good in the hood.

Can I bump thru?
Nigga come thru,
We can play 2k if you want to.

But hold up cuz you smell like weed and mom dukes not having that on the scene.
He said cool lets chill in the back I need to lay low and chill for sec.

We sat down, then he had a frown.
I looked at him and said what's going down?

Boy the shit that happened to me is the same reason why you can't be in the streets.
The hood talks and I speak the language,
A cop stopped me cuz he smelt the fragrance.

At first he didn't look like a cop,
Had a durag on, shorts and polo socks.

He walked up and said that weed is loud,
I'm tryna be lit let me cop right now.
Usually I don't sell to strangers,
My funds was low so I did him a favor.
It got sus when he asked for an ounce,
Niggas usually say how much for an ounce?

I had a funny feeling so I walked away.
He grabbed my arm and said don't walk away.
So I popped on sight
Hit em with the almighty uppercut right
Then hit em with the pistol
He was out for the count.

When he was laid out I had to run his pockets.
Took his 65 dollars and his golden locket.
Scumbag had a badge on his neck…

I stopped the convo and said you knocked out a cop?
You a dumb ass nigga,
You about to get locked.
Ohh shit earlier in the night I got stopped by the cops and they looked
kinda tight.

They asked me did I see a kid with a hoodie up pants low with a gun at
the waist.
Nigga what you said?
I said nope,
I don't talk to the feds,
I'm true to the hood and that's how you end up dead.

That's a fact but on the real, you're more than the hood
You nice at ball so get away if you could.
I got faith you gunna make it happen,
You always on the grind and you never be lackin.

Lackin out here leads to guns clapping, leading to holes in ya chest and
ya body collapsing.
The hood is my life and this shit not for you.
You my guy so I want the best for you.
Remember the feds out to get us all and they don't give a fuck whether we
rise or we fall.
We all just niggas from the hood.

Get out bro!

I told him good looks and imma do what I gotta do.
You never know, I might go to college and end up going pro.

He said that's what I like to hear,
Time is money so I gotta get up outta here.

We dapped each other up,
I said lay low and be safe.
He said this is what I do with a smirk on his face.
The hood life is something he truly embraced.

–GC

Let Me Flow

Let Me Flow with the dolphins and discover the wonders of the ocean
So I can broaden my imagination and expand my horizon.
Success is miles away,
But I'm on a speed boat fueled by knowledge
So you know I'm going 200 miles per hour.

Let Me Flow with the stereotype of a black man,
So I can prove my greatness is the opposite and take a stand.
All eyes are on me like an Obama presentation,
And all they can say surprisingly is WOW... a brother with
some education.

Let Me Flow killing ALL competition,
Because I'm a student athlete with the dedication to win.
Whether I run, jump, shoot, pass there's no doubt you'll
give me the recognition.
I follow my motto like a fan to a NBA star; Go hard and put your all in.

Let Me Flow in a raging river of reality without a life jacket
So I can fight through the currents constantly pushing me back.
I decide to dive deep in, discovering new desires in life,
Now I elevate and excel in logic and finally realized
I have essential evidence to evaluate my eager for success.

Let Me Flow with positivity
So I can neglect the negativity
And release the hostility
That may affect my possibilities
Of understanding my responsibilities
That may ahold some availability
To some outstanding opportunities...
Mind of a visionary...
I know my capabilities.

    –GC

First Infatuation

Imma tell a story on what was really real.
Back when we had fun and we could really chill.
Sitting at the lunch table never ate the meals.
Was a bad ass throwing food for the thrills.

You was always a good girl and made it happ.
Smart academy flat shoes with a gap.
I had alil crush,
You didn't care bout that.
Gre never has a chance
Go take a lap.

I never was the type of kid to quit on what I want.
Until I heard the news that Jay was the one you want.
Mixed emotions for the first I was twisted up.
Went to Jay with one intention nigga throw em up.

I had to find a way to get to you without the fight.
I asked around to all your friends about the things you like.
I went home and told my mom she gave me something nice.
Body spray with the lotion hope it made ya night.

That was the first time I had to learn,
To get what you want you have to go and earn.
Keeping you was my main concern,
Like the Knicks keeping Melo call me David Stern.

Walking thru the halls yea some months passed.
Haters always hated when we walked pass,
Like a six flags flash pass,
Like getting 90s on test and people saying how he a dumb ass.

That gotchu
So I got you
My motto was I gotchu
Anything time I went to cop something I always went and got two
Cuz I gotchu.

Separated when we got to High School.
Thought the single life would be real cool.
I was a damn fool,
Cuz I constantly thought about days we had fun and acted a damn fool.

10th grade is the year that changed my life.
We started reconnecting,
The feeling felt nice.

I remember when I got you down to the basement
And had to play it smooth.
My heart was racing the whole time before I made the move.
I sat you down on the bed to try and set the mood.
Play fighting led to me grabbing on your goods.

I gave you a perception that I had experience,
I played it smooth like I know you really feeling this.
What made it better was you didn't have experience.

There was a stare of worry in your eyes.
Laying down I felt the tremble in your thighs,
You hugged me tight looking deep within my eyes.

When you voiced softly, go slow.

Your prerogative was gentle care;
I used a delicate force,
My fear disappeared.

I entered a new world of utopia,
I wasn't sure if I was hurting ya,
The feeling that was shared can only be described as euphoria.

By the way,
That was my first time too.
I couldn't have picked a better person,
I'm glad that person was you.

The lustful interactions started turning to addiction.
We started skipping school to get our sexual fix in.
It was detrimental cuz it was ball I was missing.
Coach Granby tried to help but I didn't wanna listen.

REST IN PEACE...

Speaking of rest in peace,
I'm sorry we got rid of the *ybab* recipe.
The ingredients were somewhat cooked
Enough to see the chicken feet
But we couldn't sustain a full chicken and it haunted me.

I'm sure it was for the best...

TO BE CONTINUED...

Swag Champ

12am, we bout to start the night.
Ciroc bottles on deck, yea we just might.
Me and the team, yea we on site.
Pull up in the v your girl grilling on sight.

Swag on 100, got that Gucci Fendi Prada.
Saw this Spanish little thing who wear Balenciaga,
I hit her with some G and I told her she fire,
She said thank you
I walked away and said de nada.

Next thing you know we in the car, it's getting freaky.
She started frontin asking questions, why you wanna freak me?
Said we could have future but give me a sneak peak,
She bent over started blowing deep throating uniquely.

Turn around for them back shots.
Throw it back make ya ass rock.
I started to rip it she yelling and tripping saying give me more with that
black cock.
We switched up, she hoped on top.
She really making that pussy pop,
She going fast, I'm about to pop
I cum all over, girl clean that spot.

Now she hugging on saying that she really like me.
I know that she is a freak, I know that she is feisty.
Now she looking at me saying please don't one night me.
Held in my laugh saying you are really crazy,
I would never do that cuz honestly you amazing me.
Put her number in my phone saying make sure that I text her.
I said of course but in my head it's on to the next one,
But if a nigga horny imma make sure that I text her.

    –GC

Adolescence

I'm young and never had that before.

The essence of your ebony skin touches my flesh and instantly imports electricity electrifying positive emotion.

Emotion that makes you want to stand on top of a table that's surrounded by Victoria Secret Models and yell out ya name saying In in Lo...

Wait..

I'm young and never had that before.

The essence of your ebony skin touches my flesh and instantly imports electricity electrifying positive emotion?

Emotion that I cannot accept because there are so many Victoria Secret Models that I must seduce and offer my temporary fulfillments fulfilling fantastic fantasies of my infatuation for our future which leads to my service of sexual satisfaction.

See,

It's cuz I'm young and never had that before,
I'm young so I had to explore,
Christopher Columbus had nothing on ya boy,
Cuz all I did was explore explore and explore.
But the crazy part about it is…
No matter how much I went and explored,
You're the only one that truly had me allured.

    –GC

JOURNEY OF A MATURATION ROLLERCOASTER

Destitution

Sitting back thinking bout my town where youngins be gettin popped,
Females gettin popped,
Hooligans with no pops selling rock watching bodies drop,
That's gettin guap off the pops that deserted his daughter and baby mama
tryna get him locked.

Same daughter who uh hood chick
Dancing pop lock and drop
Yellow chick same as a box of pops.
Gettin popped off at the trap spot,
Niggas popped up tryna make it hot
Yelling WorldStarHipHop.

Up the block kid got locked.
Social Media got him yellin P.O.P hold it down
Youngin wanna be a clown
But he gotta come around and comprehend cops mission on a daily basis
is to keep the black fella down.

RIP Mike Brown.
RIP Tray Martin.
That's why we gotta stick together word to Dr. Martin.
But we steal to show off
We quick to pop off
Only time we together is when cops knock our top off.

Contradiction is how we live,
Our freedom aint what it is,
Our selves are our enemy which make us dangerous.

We are at war with who has the most
At war with who shines the most
Imma get mine are the daggering piercing words that hurt the most.

How can we get respect if we can't respect each other?
Our potential will never be met if we stay against one another.

    –GsoQ

Delhi Days

All of my niggas we put in that work,
I be in the gym and I shoot like I'm Dirk.
These hoes are so thirst
When I pull on the scene with the nudie fit jeans
Guarantee she gon twerk.

Real niggas grind til they get to the end.
Fake niggas front like they really your friend.
Scope niggas out like I'm playing Black-Ops
It's just me and dogs cuz I am legend.

I stay in the field so they calling me Geta
I'm tryna stack up and sit back with my feet up,
Never wife em cuz GQ is a cheater
I give and go my dragon ball like Vegeta.

Managing all of my thoughts;
Thought about all that I lost.
Fly through any obstacle
Cuz I'm making it at any cost.

Part 2

I walk in the club and your girl grilling me
So it's obvious that she is feeling a G.
I get her alone
Now we're all in the zone
Then she sips the Patron
She's as wet as can be.
I grab on her butt while I'm kissing her neck then she tells me to stop cuz
she think it is best.
I tell her to chill
I don't mean disrespect,
But lady let go
And I will move slow
I will give you the world and show you Pharaohs.

The psychology got her gassed in the head,
She squatted low and started giving me head,
I knocked the cooch out like Debo verses Craig.

Trusting a thot
Is like talking to cops
Never gon happen
Like it or not.

Any day your girl is bound to be taken.
They say they down actions show they be faking.
So what's the point of being in uh relation?
If I know my girl will definitely be taken.

–GsoQ

Limbo

Sometimes I don't know what my future consist of,
Cuz sometimes my vision becomes clouded by powerful doubts and
treacherous thoughts.

Sometimes I don't know what my future consist of,
So I cowardly isolate from setting goals and taking risk and creating
ideas that place me in a land of beautiful bliss.

Sometimes I don't know what my future consist of,
Because people think I'm worthless,
Is life really worth this?
There's nothing in this world I can work with!

Sometimes I don't know what my future consist of,
The reason is, cuz I honestly just don't have a clue so I'll just settle for
anything easy to do.

If you relate to this your realism needs reconstruction.

My reality related releasing realms of restriction making me reluctant to
realize my real worth.
My real reality is success, and so is yours.

So sometimes I don't know what my future consist of,
Transforms to
My consisting future is what I now do.
So what you do is true,
Because you manifest reality with the thoughts and actions you do,

Think positive people.

　　　–GsoQ

I Got the Juice

Lifted I'm touching the sky,
Gucci just looking so fly,
The chick that sit next to me I just feel on her thigh,
Cuz she got junk from behind,
Turning up lit with the crew,
I only fuck with a few,
Niggas will switch on you just like in Juice,
No one will ruin the crew,
We tight like Carter and Lee
Stars in Rush Hour 2.

You define me with a lie,
What I do you never tried,
Coward with no heart I guarantee you gunna die,
Got it so I'm gunna thrive,
I can withstand any storm,
I bring that thunder like my name is Storm,
I am a monster that takes any form,
I cannot be stopped like Pistons 04,
Damn I am on,
Call me a boss,
Like I'm Rick Ross,
Cuz I ball everyday like I'm T.Ross,
Pay me in full,
Try to Rico me I guarantee I pull the trigger I'm not with the bull,
I heard that hard work will pay off if you keep working at it day after day
after day,
But it does not take a day,
And taking off days is not in the play
Feel me!

–GsoQ

Hood Consciousness

I'm living in a world where no one cares but want the wealth.
Frauding faking taking making money but its stealth.
Cuz you low undercover Fendi on the shelf.
Yea you flexing but never considered family health.

I thought about the things I really wanna go and do.
Caused me to think about my dad and what he's going through.
Gotta put my family on my back and make it through,
So I gotta watch everything that J. Harden do.

Grandpa told me stories when he was a young blood,
Around them killers that always wanted to take blood,
Had plenty hoes that gave good neck as if they suck blood,
But the only thing that mattered was his real blood.

Sky blue feeling blue like I'm crip,
Cuz I beat a kid up got him looking crip,
I brought some blue kicks niggas think that I'm crip,
What's popping blood, 5 of them so I dipped.

Everywhere you go you constantly seeing gangs.
Gotta learn that's not the right way to really bang.
You should want to change the world and try to make a name,
But you always make it excuses and you point and blame.

What a shame,
I know the game,
I'm going crazy for the fame,
Now I'm insane,
But I'm still getting brain,
Forget her name,
Good nights of Svedk.
Zo blazing on that Mary Jane.

Ironic 2 things holding me back is women and drugs,
No smoke but I fill up the cup,
Take shots til I'm leaning and drunk,
Text shawty let me feel on ya butt,
She came thru now I'm all in her gut,

Smack on ha butt,
Pull on her hair,
Shouldn't be fair,
The way I beat the pussy up it's like I'm beating a snare,
I'm bussing a nut,
I tell her to breeze,
I realize I coulda been in the gym just putting up 3s
Damn!

   –GsoQ

Those of You

For those of you tryna make it to the top,
Tryna make the guap,
Tryna take a spot,
Tryna flow and pop;
Pursue your mission nonstop til your body drop,
Put your soul in
Follow thru Steph Curry shot.

For those of you who hate and words that relate to fake we can duke it
out bet I'll win, Alexandra the Great.
I take it back no need for harm you hate I use you as a charm you
accelerate my goal as becoming a star.

For those who got it all,
Gotta ball,
Gotta flex,
Balenciaga's Balmain or design vest;
Stunt on em,
Style on em,
Gear is your treasure chest,
Appearance is a state of mind Nas said it best.

For those of you who holding insecurities
Know the probability of your ability
Overcoming it is infinity
I hope you feeling me when I say you're gunna kill it and that's word to
Blade Trinity.

015

For those who rock it off,
Pop it off,
Knock it off!
The streets will have you arms crossed in a casket coff.
If you want to kill it
Do it with a watch and frost,
Or kill the game with a sport like you're Randy Moss.

Grind Hard!

    –GsoQ

Smooth Talk

Sit back lemme take you on a nice trip.
First off I wanna say you got some nice lips.
I'm straight forward cuz I feel you can handle it.
You a grown woman all I see is confidence.

Honestly, I can see ya secrecy.
You got a wall up don't be afraid of me,
Leave the past in the past forget about the forgery
I'm a man with strong beliefs on integrity.

And I think, that,
Ya mind is a treasure,
So believe, that,
And things will be wetter.
Damn, I mean better
But sheesh, you wetter,
Would have me deep stroking til you hitting falsetto.

I feel you woman that handles anything.
Boss lady that doesn't put up with anything.
You flawless I wish I could give you everything.
You feisty, spicy, you probably taste like everything.

You cheesing so I could tell that you feeling me.
You type the woman that can probably better me,
So the question that I'm ending with finally,
I'm in need of honey can you be my honeybee?

She started to blush,
I reach for a touch,
She's grabbing my hand and sigh and says this wasn't the plan.
I can tell that she wit it so I took it and ran.
I told her to come,
Let's go chill and have some fun.
We get out the car,
Clear sky we look at the stars.

Start talking about goals and aspirations.
Good vibes she quote, you're a revelation.
Lust leads to wet finger penetration.

Let's stop we should do it another day.
Ignored every word and continued the 4 play.
Temptations a bitch but I'm sure this the wrong way,
But a nigga horny so continued the 4 play.

She pushed me off and said you owe me an apology!
First night out and you're tryna demolish me.
I'm a star if you want me go study astronomy.
Got a question for you why you tryna astonish me?

We could be Jay & B
Living lavishly,
A power couple double trouble
Just you and me.
Apparently,
I'm J. Cole when I say we can run away and take a power trip suddenly.

I think I'm feeling you girl.

    –GsoQ

The Predicament

Obsessed with me but not of you.
Obsessed with you but not of me.

‑GsoQ

Mist

Sometimes I am lost.
In a mist of hopelessness.
Complacent in grief.

The path to success,
Seems vanquished by our feelings.
Which way should I go?

Fate navigates now.
I blindly follow my soul.
Petrified, puzzled.

What propels feelings?
The perpetrator is bad.
Bad is negative.

Negative is bad.
Also a magnet to worst.
Which evolves to hate.

Hate droughts happiness.
I will commit to real love.
The mist dissipates.

I see a bright path.
Clarity amplifies us.
But it is not all.

Someone blind can see.
With a force toward love and hope,
Goals are limitless.

Life is a journey.
Live life with a boundless mind.
Levitate nonstop.

Telling myself helps.
Cuz optimism heals all.
I am a winner.

–G. Carter

The workplace

In suspense while her back is turned he tip toes to tickle her tender firm body trusting in the fact she'll be terrified but also turned on by the tough grasp of her thigh.

She sighs in shock and sees his face and smiles and says you scared me.

He smiles then smirks then soothes her thigh with north and south seductive touch.

She halts his hand hastily then hears her boss call her name.

He walks away wallowing in lust, fantasizing on French kissing her luscious lips and lavishly licking parts of her body that'll make her reach an extremity where she's bound to cum.

He smirks and heads back to business.

–GsoQ

Triple H

The desire is an inferno that gravitates towards the ultimate one.
Countless timeless moments confirms.
No other vessel offers such utopia.
The perfect collision equates perspective expansion leading to rivers of
knowledge for thee and me and future off springs hopeful to be.

Thunderstorms rage over the once clear sky;
Eclipsing what was beautiful leading to a dark dessert of lies.
Snakes and rats devoured any lingering innocence;
Mutating a vibrant soul to a sluggish demeanor,
Mutilating commitment,
Evolving into an adulterer.

Castrated and launched into a pit of regret,
Sorrow makes the body imitate the posture of a weeping tree,
Making it hard to give genuine eye contact so there is no connect-

Shunned and exiled from intimacy,
The absence of integrity
Is happiness burglary.

The conscious thought of isolation is undesired.
So the seed of good is planted within.
With nurture the nature of the soul can be recovered and groomed to a
new utopia,
Rooting genuine intentions and blossoming euphoria.

This is the Triple H:
The Heart
The Hurt
The Hope

The recovery process of fucking someone over.

    -GsoQ

Dope Chick

Ya inner beauty vs ya booty, I don't know what's best.
Engaging conversations or licking on ya breast.
Telling terrifying tales while touching on your neck.
Talk slow to me til I find ya treasure chest.

I wanna make you feel a new way.
Like taking virginity on school days.
Touching and teasing but no toys,
My tongue do the tasting girl no noise.

Licking and licking like lollipop.
Ya clit soaking wet now come feel my cock.
This is sexual bliss not expecting resist while I'm hitting you hitting that
C note.
You deep throat,
Got me bricker than Shaq at the free throw,
Got my eyes looking crossed like I'm Debo,
Got me rolling around like its Celow.

I want you to see though,
That it ain't about sex, it's all about we though.
You constantly putting my mind on a higher level kinda sorta like
weed do.

Ya soul is amazing,
Ya heart is amazing,
Ya beauty's amazing,
Ya music's amazing,
Ya soul is amazing again,

Sit back now let's be-gin,
A journey of e-ver la-sting,
Lust that can flow into love,
No rush cuz we are two cubs,
Growing and flying we expand our horizon that transform us into
two doves,
Gross annual is above,

Society's eyes,
I promise that I,
Will grind every time,
I tell you no lie,
What's comes into truth,
While we still got youth
Persistence will equal to successful roots.

Ouoo,
I feel that you got the juice.
Ouoo,
In tune spiritual truth.
Ouoo,
Ya knowledge is ultimate power

You delicate flower,
You always devour ya music.

You hitting crescendo with easy cuz you fluent.
G I'm intrigued I feel that we congruent.
Our similarity is we're always pursuing,
And killing competition call it persecuting.

Damn girl, why you gotta be so young?

  –GsoQ

Self Questions to What?

What is it you want in life? Where do you want to be in the future? How are you going to get there? What are the steps you're going to take to get there? What are the steps you're going to take to accomplish your goal? What is your goal? If you don't achieve your goal, then what? Do you have a plan B? Or are you so confident on your plan A that you don't need a plan B? Can you make a difference in life? Why do you want success? Are you doing it for your family? Or just for yourself? If you make it, are you going to give back? What is making it? What is success? Is it a form of self happiness? What if you don't achieve anything? What will happen then? Do you get help? Or do you self analyze and get it together? Do you think of failure? Or are you so confident in your success that failure isn't an option?

WHATEVER YOU CHOOSE, WHATEVER PATH YOU TAKE, WHATEVER DECISION IS MADE, JUST KNOW, IT'S ALL ON YOU!

What will you do?

    –GsoQ

Unwind

I'm in a new place.
I think I'm the only person here from a Black race.
Does that mean I'll be placed down in last place?
Or does that mean I'm likely to catch a rape case?

However do I deal with this intense pressure?
I should lay low and move quiet like a feather,
Avoiding any attention,
This way is better,
Why am I feeling like a low case letter?

Behind The Capital, The Big, The Dominant, The Superior and The Head
of the rest.
I know there's no way I could be the best,
So I shut down letting my personality take a rest.

Wake up!
Wake up!
My soul speaks to the physical me.

Wake up!
Wake up!
The world needs to see who you are destine to be.

Wake up!
I squeeze my eyes tighter together.
Wake up!
I coil my fear tighter together.
Wake up,

To cower is selfishness to all!

I wake up,
Unwinding my cowardly ball.

Wow,
Who would have thought being yourself could gravitate so much.
This comfortability has brought happiness in a bunch,
Showing me that:

You being yourself can help another grow.
You being yourself will make you feel an internal glow.
You being yourself helps understand others.
You being yourself helps connect with your sisters and brothers.

It's ok to have fear,
But don't let it interfere with being yourself because it isn't fair.
To yourself and others around you because a lot aren't there.
Sharing who you are is the ultimate share.

    –GsoQ

The Word Search Representation
of Reflections and Changes

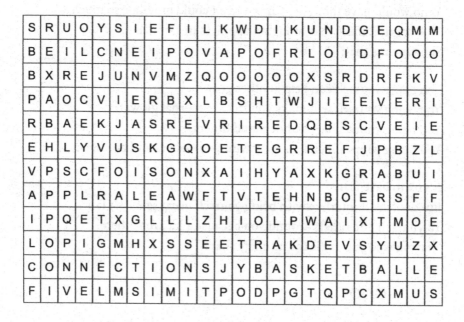

S	R	U	O	Y	S	I	E	F	I	L	K	W	D	I	K	U	N	D	G	E	Q	M	M
B	E	I	L	C	N	E	I	P	O	V	A	P	O	F	R	L	O	I	D	F	O	O	O
B	X	R	E	J	U	N	V	M	Z	Q	O	O	O	O	O	X	S	R	D	R	F	K	V
P	A	O	C	V	I	E	R	B	X	L	B	S	H	T	W	J	I	E	E	V	E	R	I
R	B	A	E	K	J	A	S	R	E	V	R	I	R	E	D	Q	B	S	C	V	E	I	E
E	H	L	Y	V	U	S	K	G	Q	O	E	T	E	G	R	R	E	F	J	P	B	Z	L
V	P	S	C	F	O	I	S	O	N	X	A	I	H	Y	A	X	K	G	R	A	B	U	I
A	P	P	L	R	A	L	E	A	W	F	T	V	T	E	H	N	B	O	E	R	S	F	F
I	P	Q	E	T	X	G	L	L	L	Z	H	I	O	L	P	W	A	I	X	T	M	O	E
L	O	P	I	G	M	H	X	S	S	E	E	T	R	A	K	D	E	V	S	Y	U	Z	X
C	O	N	N	E	C	T	I	O	N	S	J	Y	B	A	S	K	E	T	B	A	L	L	E
F	I	V	E	L	M	S	I	M	I	T	P	O	D	P	G	T	Q	P	C	X	M	U	S

Party, Sex, Basketball, Moresex, Svedka, Brotherhood, Beef,
Hardwork, Lifeisyours, Prevail, Positivity, Optimism, Love, Goals,
Connections, Breathe.

Product

I am not a product of my environment.
The environment can be the same with another but perceived differently
depending on who.

I am the way I am because of how I absorbed my environment.
I am who I am because of the mindset I've developed.
I am where I am because my mindset led me here.

Environment offers us an experience.

How you experience that environment is different from person to person,
Leading to everyone having a unique reality.

Ambition or opportunity offers you a chance to experience a
new experience.

So how you perceive that experience will determine what you are a
product of.

Leading to expansion or complacency.

So I'm a product of my mind.

    –GsoQ

Black Lives Matter/
Question to what we are

Before we get started, you must understand, all lives matter. At the same time black lives need to be respected and appreciated.

Are we a group of individuals that don't exist?
Or,
An existing group seizing back our existence?
What are we?

Are we inferior due to our skin?
Or,
Are they in fear really because of our skin?
What are we?

Are we targeted for target practice by the treacherous?
Or,
Are we tremendously tempted to traumatize the treacherous with tremendous tenacity to take what we truly deserve?

Which is:
R Respect
O Opportunity
B Balance

That spells out ROB!

We are being robbed of ROB. Ironic that were the ones with the stigma of being robbers.

You know what:

We are robbers! We rob society of their books and knowledge so we can become mentally wealthy.

We do lie! We lie our bodies in a land of deceit where we prevail against all adversity.

We do kill! We kill all competitions because we're dedicated to the top.

The fact that we are black coincides with the fact that we are back;
Back on our duty of claiming our throne,
Because we are Kings and Queens that shall never be overthrown!

So what are we?
WE ARE A GROUP OF INDIVIDUALS WITH MINDS OF OUR OWN!

BLACK LIVES MATTER!

    –GsoQ

Why are you cast out of people's mind?

You're natural curly hair sits glorified on the most simplified day.
The essence of your skin comes from cleansing soap instead of a mask
of hope.
You lack the need to cover up imperfections cuz you show a lack of need
to impress,
So I'm wondering...
How do you impress?

Is it when you decide on a day the sky is light blue with lingering white
clouds with sun rays beaming down with whistling warm winds to
sitting on a bench with a book and a turkey sandwich so in tuned into
your reading your head is down and all you see is words instead of people
strolling by?

Or are you trying to impress when you refuse to wear them short shorts
in this 78 degree weather?
You're breaking the rules here missy!
I was exposed to a world where booty shorts I mean short shorts are
worn so I can admire your features and break my neck after 3 seconds of
you passing my shoulder.

You show no interest in societies conformities.
Instead you show interest in a society that is complacent with conformity,
Leading to internal thoughts of community comradery causing
constant cultivation.
I seen ya Instagram.

I'm sorry to tell you…but your creative mind and unique behavior is not wanted here.
The powerful collude advertising a way of life to the peasants.
People want you to wear what's cool if not you're a fool.
People want you think how they think and sink what they think so you won't think to be great.
People want you to say yes and yes and yes is best cuz no means you're questioning authority and people don't do that here.

I hope you don't believe this to be true,
Your uniqueness is what makes you you.
Even though I hardly know you.

   –GsoQ

We All Have It

I walk this earth and see talent everywhere:
The singers
The dancers
The teachers
The leaders.

Talent walks with us waiting to show off anywhere:
The mall
The deli
The park
The stage.

Everywhere waits for talent to express:
With art
With sound
With movement
With tricks.

Express wants to feel what talent feels:
The pain
The joy
The sorrow
The love.

Feeling wants you to express and show off your talent
Any, and
Every,
Single,
Where.

Because the earth is your stage and we all have talent.
We would, love,
To see,
You,
Shine.

    –GsoQ

Trying to open up

Ya smooth skin strides through my mind creating strobing sparks that
seduce the body and mind. Your lips are a sweet serenade, so sweet I
become sick to my stomach. Sorry, sick refers to small butterflies, which
should summarize the feelings I've developed for you...

Time is ticking and the tale of yourself is revealed time and time again
through your tendencies. Insecurities and uncertainties restrict humans
as much as cops restrict my people. All challenges can be overcame.
The challenges you face is breaking through your poker face.

You let the world see a side of you,

But restrict the world all sides of you.

You're smarter than you'll ever know.

Ya mind has vast amounts to grow.

Here comes my insecurities...

With smarts comes deception,

As I watch I get a perception,

Of your potential, success and beauty.

At the same time the days that you are moody.

The days I don't hear from you til late,

Or day's conversations are dull,

Or days you refuse to brighten the world with your smile (which isn't often).

One thing I learned is with you nothing is impulsive besides you trying to beat me up,

So your actions always have a correlation.

We are not official but extremely exclusive in my opinion so I guess I understand ya need to fulfill ya emotional needs when I'm gone. You're exquisite so people are going to be attracted to you. Also remember the lime light is the devils playground. I'm aware there are others or another that engages you emotionally or mentally based on how you try to hide it when we are together. But the point of this was to specify how we all have flaws and trust is not present in my body. What I do trust, is the fact that I do like you, and the time I do get in your presence, I'm going to use that time and energy to make you smile and feel good.

    –GsoQ

Ylenol

Gosh dammit! Why you had to do it to me? Am I not capable? Am I
not worthy? Do I have "Do Not Commit to Him" deeply stabbed in
my back and carved into a tattoo? What the hell is it? I'm confused! I'm
puzzled! I'm lost! Is it because I briefly glanced at booty from afar? Or is
it cuz you stereotype me as a typical basketball player? If that's what is
I'll walk around with a neck brace so I won't break my neck. I'll give you
Phone! Email! Instagram! MySpace! Whatever it takes! Cuz DAMN...
All I want is commitment! I want you to be my Queen! I want you to feel
comfortable! I want you to feel beautiful! I want you to have confidence!
Cuz I'm confident in the fact that I can make you feel that way! But don't
get it twisted. I am not a YES man! Your every command you will not
here Yes Mam. Because you deserve to be challenged mentally. In this
society odds are already against you and proving your worth doesn't
come easy. And I'm here having faith in your strength and you rebuttal
with negligence... Fuck that! Imma stay true and keep this integrity
package of mine and pack my duffle bag of goodies and go. Cuz if you're
not capable of committing to another without having another... or
another and another, then you have some internal challenges you need
to face. I faced the fact that I'm not perfect. But what's fucked up is I
thought you were perfect even with your imperfections. Imperfectly
perfect...

I'm lost in a mist of agony... and it's suffocating.

It is unfortunate I don't have a real one to give me CPR.

But I'm a survivor in the cold cruel world.

So as I slowly deteriorate,

A brick wall is manufactured around me.

Now in this chimney of darkness,

I await the day I can look up and see visible light.

If you make me a believer, I may climb out,

And show you what love is all about.

    –GsoQ

Bedtime Lullaby

Cloudy skies and rainy weather.
The mood is dull and days were better.
Life is tough where nothing works.
Feeling down with painful thoughts.

Hold your head the sun is near.
Find a way the sky is clear.
Down and out to up and going.
Optimism always flowing.

      –GC

Giving

Giving is better than receiving.
Tho I received more than I gave,
I gave what I can give to the greatest of my ability.
For my ability is my talent so I give the receiver something special I
call love.

Love consist of everything,
 Or you can see it as something that consist of nothing at all,
It all depends on your mindset.
My mindset expresses love through writing.

Writing in script about dangerous trips,
Tripping bout writing causing annual dips,
Dips in the mind cuz sometimes I get lost,
Lost in the bliss of the negative thoughts.

I thought so negative, I, too seen love as nothing at all,
All because I refused to open up when love came knocking on my door.
The door became a nuisance from loves boom boom bang,
I bang on an empty Honey Nut Cheerios box 3 times, boom boom bang
crushing it completely yelling out I hate that noise and stood up.

Stand for something or fall for anything I say to myself as I approach
the noise.
The noise of love goes boom boom bang, and my hate unleashes a boom
boom bang,
Then BANG...!
It hit me that love and hate produce the same sound so it must come
from the same place.
So I place my hand on the handle deciding to let love in.

Once inside love conquered all locking hate into solitude.
I solidify love with appreciation increasing its magnitude.
I am a magnet attracting in a positive attitude.
I hope this attitude helps the receiver show gratitude.
If not gratitude hopefully you reach a better latitude.

Cuz a latitude that comprehends love and appreciation,
Will see the act of giving as a form of recreation.
Let's recreate the act of giving.
Because we all deserve to receive something from love.

    –GsoQ

My Delicate Rose

I want your soul.
Your mind,
Your body,
Your heart,
I won't let anything to tear us apart,
Because we're growing seeds destine to blossom into two beautiful
rose petals.

Your animal passion gives me a glimpse into your soul revealing a sacred
connection to compassion.

You care for all because your heart is made of gold and your pure soul
can never be sold,
To the dark force full of corruption and false beliefs.
Your advocacy to the unnoticed exposes your bravery,
Making you a descendent of Athena.
Goddess of a heroic nature.

Baby you are a bonafide blooming bold
Brilliant brave breathtaking beautiful bliss
Of a person and the best thing happening to me.

You are the fire to my candle,
Expanding my horizon giving me light and
Guidance to a brighter future.

I've made it my priority to open your
Hidden gates to bring forth the ultimate
Sense of comfortability I desire from you so much.

I see your potential and will patiently wait to unwrap the rest of your
preserved prettiness.

We will dance
We will laugh
We will bath in the bath.
We will cry
We will try
We will strive for the sky.
We will grow
We will show
And instinctively know,

That this is for real,
And my love for you is truly forreal.

    –GsoQ

IT DOESN'T MATTER

Before we get started viewers must understand I'm speaking in context
of the humanistic approach. I'm fully aware of the inequality going on in
this world.

It doesn't matter that she is a woman,
She'll thrive under any circumstances a man could do.

It doesn't matter that he is white,
Skill is skill and you'll get served if you're game isn't right.

It doesn't matter that he is a male,
He can be a parent without help from the mother still.

Guess what,
Your sexual orientation,
It doesn't matter!
Girl to Girl,
Girl to Guy,
Guy to Girl,
Guy to Guy,
If you don't accept it
Please ask yourself why.
Look in the mirror and regurgitate your thought,
I read minds so I'm telling you, you sound silly.
Ignorance isn't bliss.

The truth is really this:

All white blondes aren't ditzy.
All homeless people aren't filthy.
Not all Muslims cause terror.
People out of jail can do better.

All Black people don't steal.
All elderly people aren't ill.
People with disabilities have abilities too.
Who are you to say what they can and cannot do?
This world has put disability on the back burner,
So it's time to put them on a pedal stool.
Inclusion is the best gift we can offer.

All cops aren't corrupt.
All white people aren't rich.
Not every Black person eats fried chicken.

The fact that I loved a White woman being a Black man should have
no relevance.

The stereotypes in this world makes things matter,
When they absolutely SHOULDN'T MATTER!

Which causes bias decisions,
Which takes the control and opportunity away from
qualified individuals,
Which leads to an imbalance of power,
Which is inequality,
Which causes resentment,
Which brings segregation,
What happened to being one nation?

IT DOESN'T MATTER WHAT YOU ARE,
It's a matter of WHO YOU ARE WITHIN.

There's no such thing as normal.

     –GsoQ

SUNYAC CHAMPS CSTATE

We the Red Dragons C state,
Got damn we real great,
Spectators all hate
Cuz all the 3s that we make.
Rell in the lane jumping high like he Griff Blake,
We gotta stack team we the champs, yea we all great.

Shayne to the lane,
Throwing up floaters.
Blair with the 3 don't let em half court cha.
The range is insane,
Now J-Mo in the game,
Hit the pull up 3 last second we win the game.

G to the Q don't let em shift and shake ya,
Money make ya,
Go to the rim and take ya.
We got JP guarantee he pump faked ya,
Went to the lane and laid ya,
See ya later.

He got the skat too.
Kellz got it too.
Mr. Right hand nation flying right by you.

Zay playing smooth.
Terrence got the moves.
Carrel killing cats still inna bad mood.

Dan the man pull up 3
Travis Heff the man to be
He doing everything elite,
J-Riv young as hell but stronger than a wildebeest,
Coop game never weak,
Lay me package kinda neat,
Andrew got the spot up 3.

Andre Hampt., hard worker, shot stroker;
Tripping thru the lane and making funny looking floaters.
Jeff plays strong don't sleep he will work ya.
Zack Attack had the skat, get better soldier.

Mo Blocka, coach player will stop ya;
Hit you with a screen, Coach Heff with the chopper.

Quote of the year, if it's one game we winning…It's this one;
Coach Hodge said it yea he real fun.

Pat Swayz got the juice for managing phenomenal.
Luck say stack and move, post up chronicles.
Coach Span talking budget
And make it sound logical.
Shooters on shooters, Cstate still unstoppable!

We out here!
Shout out to my guys Paul, Prenda, Mike Graney, Eamonn and Wiz.
SUNYAC CHAMPS BABY!
Wooooo!

    –GsoQ

Letter to Basketball

Dear Basketball,

This is a surreal moment for me right now. I finally accomplished one of my goals. I WON A BASKETBALL CHAMPIONSHIP WITH MY SCHOOL. It feels amazing. I feel like I hit the lotto. God, I just wanted to thank you, you and I both know how much I wanted this. Winning this championship, matter fact, playing in this season made me realize a lot about myself. I'm 100 percent meant to lead and inspire people. Being a captain and being put in predicaments where I had to do those things made me realize it. I love basketball and I always will love basketball. I have a lot of skill and knowledge of the game, but I'm at a point in my life where I need to move on and accomplish another one of my goals. Despite this extremely difficult decision, I'm pretty sure it's what's best. Basketball will always be a part of my life. I came to a reality that I will not play professional basketball. Not because I don't have enough skill because I definitely do but because I'm realizing I'm not a completely dominant in game player right now. I mean there's one hundred and one justifications but I also have lots of other aspirations. It took more than a lot for me to just say what I said two sentences ago, I deleted it probably four times. I guess you can say I'm growing up where I have to make lucrative decisions now. I'm going to take a new path where my dedication doesn't revolve around basketball yearly like it has for the last 5 years of my life. Once again this is very difficult but change must occur. I want to see where life takes me without basketball. I'm excited and nervous at the same time. One thing I learned from basketball is I must stay positive and optimistic and that's what'll do. Thank you basketball for giving me closure and ending this chapter of my life on a positive note. I love you!

2/28/16 1:09am

–GsoQ

11:16am at Raquette Lake

Ma I want you to see this.
Ya little bald headed one big tooth having batman suit wearing boy has
grown up.
Grown up so much sometimes I feel like I can touch the sky.
I know you can't literally touch the sky,
But I developed this mindset that takes me on journey of consciousness
where I'm above all of the bullshit.
Sorry for the vile language,
But we're from a place where vile is oxygen,
Inhaling toxic negativity that makes you cringe into a ball because that's
all there is to breathe in.
The best part about breathing is, you don't inhale what you exhale.
You inhaled the negative and exhaled positivity,
They unveiled plague snatching away opportunity,
He revealed rage leading to ya carnal availability.
Now it's just me and you... but you still took the responsibility.
You're my superwoman.
Like you, I have an S on my chest for success,
But succeeding is nothing without serenity.
So this is for you Dad.
With this mindset I manifested maturity,
Making moves to monopolize my mind to increase the magnitude
of making million dollar ideas to make sure my magnificent family
members live a marvelous life!
And that's mostly because of you.

I look back and I pack my bag holding my basketball in my right arm anticipating a guaranteed arrival time of 8:30.

Ready to show off my skills I sit at the edge of the bed repeating in my head in and out cross, in and out cross, in and out cross, which was my favorite move. I was an above average 11 year old player. I thought you knew that too. I go in the kitchen to look at the microwave, one of the only resources for time. It was 8:29. The eagerness was similar to Christmas Eve at 11:59 when mommy said I can open that one gift I was eyeing. I skip back to the room and laid down on my pillow case that had two skinny flat pillows and an old folded t shirt in it for cushion, because I felt butterflies in my stomach, nervous about the one on one game I knew was gunna take place. The park lights cut off at 10 but I knew you'd be there so I closed my eyes for a quick nap. I woke up and checked the time again......

As I walked back to my room, mommy stopped me and asked me "what's the matter?" I never liked for mommy to see me in a fragile state as if I just got stood up on a first date, so I picked my head up from my chest, looked her in the eye and said… I'm good. Having you not show up 20 plus times does a toll on you.

But look at the bright side I also remember the time you came to my basketball game in Rockland County. It was the championship game and my team was the underdog. You was right by my side saying Gre you gunna kill em, Do You! It was like every time I heard those words I became superhuman and I had no worries. Game time started and I had tunnel vision. I was hitting shot after shot after shot and you were running up and down the sidelines as if you were the ref. They even had to stop the game to tell you to settle down.

And after every made basket there you were yelling at the top of your lunges saying YEA THAT'S MY G!
That was one of the greatest moments in my life.

So with this mindset Dad...
I just wanted to let you know... I forgive you.

    –GsoQ

Conversation of maturation

So I met this individual,
When I felt invincible.
Seen him on the scene with a black power visual.
Asked him what's the sign about?
He huffed and said incredible,
Another black nigga lacking knowledge shit is pitiful.
How the fuck I'm pitiful?
I'm not into politics but I can get political.
I know about the Sean Bells the Mike Browns it's critical.
Understandable but you gotta understand that falls under typical.
If we talk political,
We talking bout authority and how they're not credible.
They think they have superpowers like the Incredibles.
Luring in the innocent and killing individuals.
And they get residual
For locking kats up to meet a quota it's despicable.
A present change happening sounds really mythical.
Gotta approach this situation with some strong principles.

I get it...so what you saying is we gotta get physical?
Looked at me and said no avoid being typical.
Remember their perception is they see us as criminals.
Animals,
Some see us as cannibals.
So we have to be strong like the Manimal,
Together like a band would do,
Loyal to impeccable enhancables.
Enhancables?
I'm talking about intelligence to be invincible,
Defendable,
Admittable,
Convincible,

This mindset needs to be traditional,
Feel me bro?
Let's start local then start moving national,
The ultimate goal is to move to international,
Sounds a bit much and it may sound irrational,
Manifest a strong mind we can make it rational.
BUT IT STARTS WITH YOU!

If you don't go and do, our people are through.
So what must I do?
Spread all of the truth
To the youth,
And realize
You can be
Anything
You want to be

But you gotta see
Nothing is E.Z.
So you gotta grind
Be divine,
Tell yourself you gunna make it and shine
No need for crime,
Focus up and in a matter of time
You'll draw a line,
Pledging to the best intuitive mind
The holy prime.

I got it!
Imma find my path,
Then help out another.
Imma spread knowledge,
Show love like a brother.

Imma grind,
Imma shine,
Imma manifest a storyline,

That shows no matter how much negativity is in this world,
The columbine,
The hate crimes,
The money slimes,
We can all still commit to personal accountability to reaching
gold mines.

Which is a goal mind.
Even if you go blind,
The path to success is saw by solidifying the appreciation of life.
We then become sanctified.
Unity is all!

Wow that was deep!
Facts!

–GsoQ

Ohana

Let our bond be unbreakable and our love be inseparable.
Our pursuit to happiness consist of comradery and showing empathy.
If we happen to show sympathy,
Let comfort and care be the epitome of our daily living overcoming
any catastrophe.
We are a unit,
A team,
A fraternity.
We are one.

No one is left behind.
No one is left alone.

Our uniqueness tenacity and integrity is what keeps us strong to
the bone.

We. Are. Family.

        –GsoQ

Ohana Part 2

ZO, I remember way back when we use to ball in the backyard til our hands were black from dirt and the sky went from light blue to yellow to orange to purple. We would go inside and feast on microwaveable beef patties. I was always jealous when you put cheese in yours so I had to imitate you. We were brought up together and I looked up to you. You had PAL on smash and witnessing that lifestyle, ignited the confidence in me to live a movie life no matter where I was at. I'll always consider you a brother!

Teonna, you're tremendous from cranium to the toe. You're definitely the strongest female I know. Literally! Every time we play fight I either end up with a scratch from your tiger claw nails or some type of whelp on my arm. You've been my ride or die from the time I drew you as a clown causing you to burst into tears and saying "Never again will I be your friend! NEVER!" To the times we use to dig holes in the backyard and see how many worms we can find. To the times I use to watch you make slides from your bunkbed with your pee mattress. To the times I called you about my relationships and adventures.

Domo, the dominant dope artist destine to greatness. You're my little bro and I watched you grow. From young, I seen your advance rapping, reading, rationale ability and I always wanted success for you. I always told you confidence will take you a long way. Whether your path of life consist of rapping or engineering music I have faith/hope that you'll embrace any challenge and show the world the genius you are.

Jennay, you're the nosiest person in the world! When I reflect upon your personality, ultimately I realize you ask all these questions because your compassion for the family and your love for others trumps all boundaries where you want to ensure others meet the qualification to be a part of our unity. I love you with all my heart and thank you for helping me grow and supporting me throughout all stages of my life.

Mama, you're my spiritual sansei. Our souls are connected. We are in tune with the higher power which will give us the ability to travel the cosmos, explore galaxies, thrive in solar systems and appreciate the worlds of life. My perspective has grown and my energy has strengthen due to your influence. You will be the Sun, sharing your energy to all. I love you!

Granddaddy/GP, you're the father I always wanted. You've constantly provided guidance when I truly needed it. You showed me how to be a smooth criminal, as well as how important it is to give to others. You make the world smile with your personality and ability to engage others. You're the head of the family and know your wisdom has shaped a better man in me, Alonzo, Rahece, Domo and I'm positive, many more. I love you.

Kora, as I reflect on your soul, you're one of the most caring, giving and genuinely compassionate individuals in our family. We grew up together and you're a tough cookie because you were tortured by either me or Alonzo or the both of us. Oh yea and we can't forget about kitty. He use to tear your leg and arm up. Despite all of the old fun and games, I will always love you and be there for you no matter what.

Keyara, you're going to my little baby sister whether you're 17 or 70! I don't know what it is, but I have this instinctual feeling to always want to protect and want the best for you. I take much pleasure in knowing you have already developed a phenomenal mindset and you're going to thrive at anything you pursue. If modeling or hair styling is your calling, obsessively manifest it through thought and verbiage and it shall be yours. Research Law of Attraction.

Faith, loyalty is a lost trait in this society. You are the epitome of a loyal soul, and have been in my life since I was a Gerber. You're a flower that has blossomed an animated personality and ability to care for others. Bubbling Brown Sugar til the end!

Kendal, you're a very dramatic animated talented fun beautiful smart young lady. I see a part of me within you when it comes to leading. You always want to assist me when I'm facilitating family activities and sometimes you come up with some great ideas. Keep learning and let your creative juices flow. And alllllways remember, Teonna is a living troll doll and Keyara isn't going to have any teeth at 30 because she eats 30 Dubble Bubble gums in a day.

Rahece, you're the warrior of the family. Your international stories confirm you've lived a movie life. Welcome to the club lol. On the real, I admire your fatherhood. Your off springs will accomplish nothing but greatness. Continue to treat your wife like a Queen! Your kids are very fortunate to see those interactions and it'll inspire them to do the same.

Mother/Muñeca, you are the GOAT!!!

I LOVE YOU ALL. I'M BLESSED TO HAVE SUCH AMAZING SOULS IN MY LIFE!

    -G. Carter

Universal Care

The betterment of mankind happens when one cares for another.
Caring comes in all shapes and sizes, giving everyone the opportunity
to express.
The continuity of care gives everyone a significant other,

Which gives relief to individuals in distress.
Those who are lonely sad mad tired done hurt ignored abused and every
other exhausting emotion,
Care helps put distress to rest, offering a delicate genuine support like a
gentle caress.

Care is entitled to the happy proud silly grateful blessed honest loved and
every other positive devotion;
Because it is an epitome of a universal offering with no
discriminating attributes.
So let's minimize seeing care as a commotion;

Failing to see what care constitutes.
The act of care can be expressed to individuals with no relation,
So care should have infinite distributes.

Caring has a kindness to all correlation.
We all deserve care from somewhere;
Understand your care can help another reach a more
uplifting destination.

    –GsoQ

Homeless

Sitting down on a black empty crate on a New York sidewalk I hold up a
cardboard sign that says,
I'm a low class man looking for intimacy.

Back hedged over
Head down
My cardboard sign to the world is held on my left thigh waiting to
be noticed.

I've been sitting here for so long I smell of a decomposed corpse due to
my internal damages and rotten organs.
Specifically the heart and the brain.

The heart was stabbed lost broken denied taken and never fully
accompanied with another heart.

Causing the brain to constantly shutdown mentally, finally resulting in
loss of hope, loss of faith, and now a loss of feeling.

Those who approach my sign I no longer look up.
Slumped over
Head down
I say in a tired lamenting voice…
Show me what you got.

I have heard seen felt and done it all so I'm sure our cycle will lead me
back to this black empty crate.
But still give me what you got,
My physical pleasures can be met and I'm sure I can find your spot.

This cardboard sign isn't about sex.
It is about achieving intimacy which complements absence of neglect.

So as you pass by noticing me
Slouched over
Head down
With a cardboard sign,

Out of respect keep it moving if you don't have an intimate state of mind.

    –GsoQ

REAL

I'll be real,
My defensive mechanism is to never believe still.
Because if I believe and happen to be deceived
It'll put me at a state where I would constantly grieve.
I don't wanna grieve.
Wearing my heart on a sleeve is like being under water and trying to breathe;

So God gave me gills,
And told me you'll need them if you seek to accomplish real.
Does real mean I have to express how I feel?
God responded with you'll be surprised with the results and it may seem surreal.

My fidelity is in falsity commitments so I'm drowned by fear.
God said you have lungs and gills so fear no more and dare to be real.

Now I'm on a precipice lamenting over the duplicity I've experienced.
God said don't dwell on an experience you had to experience.
What you experienced will guide what you experience,
But the mind dictates how you experience.
Approaching all with positive will give sight to real.
Slapped by anger I rebuttal but all aren't real!

God responds one's sight and path to real is individualized,
But we all are one so how you accept real will affect another.

This is a dogma.

The battle with one's self can only be won with acceptance,
So I surrender…
Giving up fear.
And was reeled in by real.
I hold on to a railing propelling myself up to hear God say:

Real is strength,
And
Strength is you.

   –GsoQ

First Infatuation Part 2

I had a couple offers to go play away in college.
Mentally I wasn't there, and cared less about a college.

Thankfully you were there and had the proper mind.
You made me think about the future,
You helped me see an inner shine.

Thanks to you we both ended up at SUNY Delhi.
It honestly was a gift and a curse.

Gift cuz I still had you by my side,
Jr. High to college was a hell of a rollercoaster ride.
College was something new and you were still my ride or die.

Curse cuz I was cursed as a beast.
A wild scavenger looking for the finest treat.
There was so much to choose my brothers and I always feasted.

My curse put our relationship in a hearse.
You stayed true trying to get us back on course.
My curse put our relationship in a hearse.
Humiliation and rumors overwhelmed you.
My curse put our relationship in a hearse!
You experienced spiritual and emotional neglect.
My curse put our relationship in a hearse.
Fed up you retaliated showing karmas force.

The hearse was miles away and my curse of the beast still lingered.
Time passed and I became haunted by the reminiscence of abuse I inflicted,
Creating an urge to offer you a better me.

You're a tough cookie.

Despite our history, as years passed our connection wasn't
fully diminished.
Spontaneous contacts from either you or I showed our time
wasn't finished.

My hopes for reuniting changed by the season
And the fact that we spoke like best friends didn't make letting go easy.

It is selfish to hold on;
Selfish to ourselves,
And
Selfish to others.

So maturation turned history into history,
Vanquishing the anchor of hope,
Unlocking the door to the soul,
Releasing a refurbished heart.

My ship has sailed.

Change the world with your smile.
Change the world with your inner drive.

And let the ocean of optimism bring you currents of perseverance
Exposing you to beautiful coastlines.

Peace and Prosperity.

Your first,

        –G. Carter

Liaverp Cycle

Everything moves in perpetual motion
As everything moves whether you like it or not.
Sight of an eagle overpowers the sight of a bat
Offering a clearer vision to a happier state.
So dwelling on experiences that failed to be great
Will place your body and mind in a negative state.
Committing to that path will lead to a negative fate.

Stray away,
I'm telling you there is a better way.
The optimistic yellow brick road has many paths all leading to The
Positive Bay.

Swim with hope regardless of high or low tides.
Non swimmers let the force of hope be your boat ride.

During the hurricane your life jacket is your jacket of faith,
So take on any tsunami and prepare to be great.
Confidence
Consistency
Commitment,
Are the 3 Cs of Positive Cultivation
Giving you the mindset to overcome anything, which leads to
limitless destinations.

You now become a showcase of inspiration.
People will view your mindset as motivation.

This process becomes a cycle of prosperity.
The goal is to spread this mindset universally.
The moral of the story is:

Sky's the limit when you prevail against any adversity.

    –GsoQ

First Love

I miss you so much.
The more time I spend away,
The more I feel I need you in my life.

You never handed me anything.
You made me work for everything.

You made me feel like an adventurous kid that sat in the front first seat
of a rollercoaster giving me sight to a beautiful surrounding as it rises,
the exhilarating feeling when feeling speed when performing acrobatic
spins and changes of directions, the fabulous euphoric feeling of feeling
afraid of false safety while flying freely in the air for a few moments and
trusting in the fact those few seconds are freedom.

To you I gave my blood sweat and tears.
To you I sacrificed many years.
To you I swore when together I will prevail through the fears;
Until there is no fear.

You are what I am,
You are what I do,
I will always be with you,

Basketball, I love you.

      –G. Carter

I AM A VESSEL

A vessel to greatness
A vessel to life
A vessel to success
A vessel to realization.

A vessel of attraction
A vessel of lust
A vessel of love
A vessel of feelings.

A vessel for goals
A vessel for visions
A vessel for creativity
A vessel for theories.

A vessel with appreciation
A vessel with inclusion
A vessel with sharing
A vessel with equality.

A vessel always encouraging
A vessel always motivating
A vessel always positive
A vessel always growing.

A vessel without hate
A vessel without pessimism
A vessel without cruelty
A vessel without disrespect.

A vessel that makes mistakes
A vessel that learns from mistakes
A vessel that works hard
A vessel that never quits.

A vessel who dances
A vessel who plays
A vessel who laughs
A vessel who does.

A vessel you know
A vessel you see
A vessel you knew
This vessel is you.

–G. Carter

D.A.B

The most manipulating person I've ever met in my life. There's so much natural talent in her it's ridiculous. She sees the world as her canvas and utilizes utensils as her form of expression.

Fearless indeed she is for taking on challenges is sport to she. I now speak directly to thee pronouncing thee Queen of Creativity.

Now here me through rhythm because your mind is a temple.
You're light years from ordinary making beautiful seem simple.
Your gifts to the world are sip and paints that impacts on a ripple.
I watch in shadows causing raindrops to trickle.

Raindrops represents the sorrow I produce.
My mind knows together unlimited will produce.
Like putting the batta to the bang or the drip to the drop or the hip to the hop
Our connection is spiritual like the Noah's Ark.

Our connection is deep like marrow in the bone,
Beautiful like the sight of the Milky Way,
Strong like the sun,
Consistent like a heartbeat.

I am a fool for ignoring my heart.

I am a fool for hurting your heart.

Lust and temptation together breed an untamable beast with no consciousness of feelings for others…

The only tamer is Maturation.

Simba to Nala,
Mickey to Minnie,
Princess Jasmine to Aladdin,

Belle to the Beast.

We are two characters from different tales of life destine for an unforgettable story.

But sorry,
I cannot give you what you need.

–GsoQ

Mi Yrros Fi

I'm sorry if I couldn't give you my all;
I'm sorry if I failed to give you a call.

I'm sorry if I didn't respond to your text;
I'm sorry if we had sex then I left.

I'm sorry if I don't remember your name;
I'm sorry if you experienced my games.

I'm sorry if I ever told you a lie;
I'm sorry if I ever made you cry.

I'm sorry if you ever thought we were real;
I'm sorry if you ever paid for my bill.

I'm sorry if you thought we could be;
I'm sorry if you lost faith in me.

I'm sorry if we ever went on a date;
I'm sorry if I showed up kind of late.

I'm sorry if I never took you out;
I'm sorry if I never figured you out.

I'm sorry if your relationship is ruined;
I'm sorry if I made you say damn he blew it.

I'm sorry if you never met my mom;
I'm sorry if I never held your palm.

I'm sorry if I was ever unfaithful;
I'm sorry if I was ever ungrateful.

I'm sorry if I said sorry so often.
I'm sorry...so I put the old me in a coffin.

–GsoQ

ANXIETY

What if she meets another guy that has more money than me and ends up accepting the invitation of a cool excursion that leads to her being so infatuated that she ends up having sex with that person?

What if I decide to open up to her and give her my all and she responses saying she loves me, meanwhile she's having an affair with her co-worker?

What if I choose the wrong wife?

What if I end up getting married because I believed she was the one I'm supposed to be with and then end up getting a divorce within 5 years?

What if the girl I thought I was going to marry ends up marrying someone else?

What if I end up having a child with someone that I don't seek a permanent future with?

I want my wife to be independent where she relies on her mind to get ahead.
Expressive to the point she can share her viewpoints whether it's through talking, writing or the arts.
Adventurous where she's comfortable with experiencing spontaneous moments and places with me.
Freaky where sex is passionate, kinky and our bed is where we make it.
Committed by having integrity and remaining faithful to me and our family.
Supportive by motivating me to keep going, inspiring me to constantly grow and giving me positive energy when I'm down.

My future wife I will give you my all,
Mind Body and Soul.
I will treat you like a Queen,

Fill your heart with genuine love,
Tell you and make you feel that you are beautiful,
Challenge your mind with dope conversations,
And give you the confidence that you can trust me.

In my head we live in our own world.
No one can disrupt what we have,
No one can stop us from doing us,
No one can change how we act toward each other.
No one can understand one another how we understand one another,
Because what we have is something called a connection.
And the connection with the one you are supposed to be with, is the
most vibrant connection of them all.

I didn't want to be in a relationship,
I think I understand now.

I didn't know what I wanted.
I didn't want to connect with another.
I just wanted to reap the benefits of what a connection brings.

To overcome you must constantly learn thy self
Love thy self
Be thy self
So you can love another and another can love thee.

This is a scary stage of life.

But
What would you do for REAL LOVE?

      –G. Carter

Graduation Attendance

It doesn't make sense why you continuously say you're going to do something...and then you don't do it! What was the point of even saying it? Are you trying to make me feel better by using words you think I want to hear? The reality is those words mean ABSOLUTELY NOTHING to me! To the point it makes me infuriated to even hear you speak. I heard it ALL. I'm going to do this! I'm going to do that! That's my word I'll be there! I got you! I GOT ME! So all of the times you put my hopes up, all of the times you led me to believe, all of the times you let me down, all of the neglect that led to my grief, I absorbed that bitch as fuel to spark up all I achieved! We are a dichotomy, for your lack of attendance, parenthood and integrity, has fueled a monster DESTINE for greatness!

...I thought I was at a good place with you mentally.

    -G. Carter

Tori's Kings

I was a young boy living in the town of Hollis Queens,
Where Russell Simmons started pushing crack to dope feens,
Where I threw rocks at moving cars and hid behind trees,
Met my first Queen where I lost my vir-gin-ity,
Ouuu Wee!

I can take you back to the time where I had to witness my older bro
do time,
For a high speed chase he always thrived doing crime
We use to watch street ball
In the yard we would grind.

I remember PAL,
He use to give em hell.
I remember Jr. Knicks
When he got his first chip.
He hit the game winner
Granddad was super lit,
I remember Marilyn
In the room he would hit.

Fast forward a couple years I ended up away at college.
Brother told me don't follow him and get my knowledge.
I got my knowledge,
By playing ball and getting hoes and getting grades that managed to get
me to graduation day.

Just because I did it that doesn't mean that I'm finished
The grind is always infinite
My mind is wired to get it
To stop is always illicit
My actions always explicit
I have tripping days but never lose sight of the only mission;

Which is growth,
For me.
And growth, for you.
And growth for Tori and Alyasha Williams too.

Cuz we are blood,
And we have starved,
So we
Had to
Go get
Our grub.

Don't worry my brother, imma do everything in my power to make sure
I set a great example for Tori.
I'm honored to be her God Father.

Congratulations on another successful birth with Alonzo the IV.

    –G. Carter

Eye em Who Eye em

The hood me vs the professional me
The cool me vs the quiet me
The confident me vs the negative me
The intelligent me vs the unaware me.

The romancer or the player?
The athlete or the writer?
The domestic or the adventurer?
The assertive or the passive?

The analyst
The arrogant
The obsessive
The overprotective?

Orrrr

The committed
The cheater
The consistent
The charismatic?

Do you choose?

My hoody or my blazer?
My snapback or my fedora?
My cargos or my corduroys?
My sneakers or my shoes?

Whatever you choose,
Just know that you lose
If you think one of the above is not something I was.

I am who I am
And stand for who I am
Because all of the above is what makes me who I am.

Take it or leave it,
I am who I am.

      –G. Carter

Pariah Prerogatives

Take a second and tell yourself you are blessed.
You can hear
You can read
You can see
You can hold the object you are holding to see and read this piece.

Take a second and tell yourself you are blessed.
You can walk
You can talk
You can control your movements
You can make choices for yourself.

Take a second, go back to the beginning and put a (t) after all of the (Cans) above.

Only pick 4 Cants.
The other 4 you still possess.

Tough decision?

Are you still blessed?

It is definitely a tough decision when you possess all of the above.
Which is the reason why you shouldn't take life for granted.

More importantly you should be aware that there are individuals in this world that do not have all of those abilities.

That doesn't make them ANY less blessed than you or me.

Their lives are special and unique.

If their reality relies on assistance for well-being then so be it!

We ALL require help in some way,

We ALL are entitled to assistance,

So we ALL need to play a part.

Whether it's inclusion advocacy empathy or simply deciding to treat ALL as your equal,

Your duty to act is essential.

The mind is a beautiful thing and just because your way of thinking or communication is different from another,

Shouldn't lower the value of someone else's life.

Cherish another how you would want to be cherished, for the survival of mankind relies on it.

   –G. Carter

Don't Lose Your Power

I almost lost my way.
I started thinking about living for the money instead of living for
my passions.

I almost kept my focus on the future and forgot about the present.
I almost started to doubt my success.

All that I can be
Can only be generated by all that I can see.
Not with my eyes, but with my mind.

My mind is a powerful tool that can fix any problem and bring
forth solutions.
So I visualize what I want until that want becomes a reality.

Sometimes I get what I want immediately,
Sometimes I get what I want in a couple of days,
Sometimes I get what I want within weeks,
Sometimes it takes months for me to get what I want.
Even years!

Cough Cough, College Basketball Championship!

The secret behind it is I never gave up on what I wanted no matter how
long it took.

Still til this day I won't give up on my pending goals.

Don't get me wrong,
Circumstances happen and goals do change.

But the foundation of achieving what you want comes from an obsessive thought of that specific desire.

Try it!

    –G. Carter

Old Language of Love

Tackled by belligerency
Thy fellow man equates love with destitution;
Arguing thee who love are chained to misfortune and bound to doom.

Thou shall not kill now brothers thou shall not love.
It is a sin;
An unforgivable act.

But love is not only act.
It is the burning desires,
The vivid dreams,
The integrity of formed relationships.

Absence of love
Is presence of subterfuge.

Thou can live and do and ditto falsity.
But those are empty vessels;
The living dead.

True is love.
Love is true.

Be true to love,
And love will be true to thee.

–G. Carter

Diamond in a Ruff

Ohh Diamond in a Ruff,
I am misconstrued by pebbles in the soil.
I stop to graze upon a stone to puzzle together a type.
Igneous
Sedimentary
Metamorphic.
My obsessive self dreads but enthusiastically lifts the stone from the soil
to brush away lingering dirt.
Ouu La La, an igneous.
I admire I desire I cherish this igneous and put it on display.
I say to myself this igneous has come from a volcanic darkness so I offer
all of my light in the most passionate way...
But what about me?

Ohh Diamond in a Ruff,
You as well were discovered in the dirt.
Covered with blood with mud with tar, but immediately brushed off
revealing a diamond shiny star.
Swiftly I knew how auspicious you would be.
Not solely for your divinity and grandiosity,
Surely for the unique nuance of emotion and interaction that has brought
light to me.
So much,
I want to be your luminosity.

The effect of me shining on you is a glistening diamond shining on me;
A reciprocal shine destine for eternity.
This is the goal of life.

We are the complementation of two worlds revolving each other.
Each with exquisite uniqueness.
The epitome of a rock solid connection.

I'm in love with you.

-G. Carter

My Duty of Pleasure

Standing up I look her in the eyes while grasping both hands on her booty.

I pull her in closer.

Now her breast press upon my chest.

I feel her warmth as she feels mine.

I gently lift her chin and begin to kiss her lips.

I bite her bottom lip and invite her to my tongue.

She greets me with a circular motion of her tongue while my pointer finger gently plays with her clit.

She is wetter than a waterfall and I am harder than a rock,

But it is not time for penetration so I continue to tickle her spot.

I lift her in the air and she wraps her legs around my back.

Seductively I lick and bite her neck,

Then I throw her on the bed and lift both legs to her shoulders.

I pleasure her clit, by writing in script, this pussy is mine with my tongue as I'm spreading her lips.

She grabs on my head as I'm licking her clit and simultaneously finger fucking her soul.

I look up at her and smile, then bite my lip.

Now let the games begin.

–G. Carter

To My Offspring

I promise to be the best father I can be.
You deserve to be *loved* and cher*i*shed and guided to a path of greatness.

I will be your support system through the bad and horri*f*ic, as well as the te*r*rific and explicit.

Everyth*i*ng I'll do will be beneficial for you;
Even if it *is* a challenge hard for you to do.

You'll hear me say sky's the limit when you prevail against adversity
A LOT.
That statement guide*d* me through lif*e*,
So *s*ay *i*t to yourself when entan*g*led in a tough predicament and utilize it
to get you out of that k*n*ot.

I will t*e*ach you what I know as you will teach me what I *d*o not know
and what I do not know I will learn to know so you can know that I
know.
What you do not know never he*s*itate to say you do not know so you
learn what you did not know which will lead to you knowing.

Life is a *puzzle* with easy pie*c*es and di*ff*icult p*i*eces, but know all of the
pie*c*es *a*re there for you to put together.

*L*ife is a*l*l about learning and experiencing, and I can't wait to experience
it with *y*ou.

I will *fi*ll y*our* soul with wisdom,
I will give you my all my child.

I love you!

Now find the hidden message,

Please and thank *you*.

 -G. Carter

The Siren

Oh shit!
What did I do?
Who died?
Who got shot?

There's the Red White and Blues, let's get off this block.
I'm trying to avoid getting noticed and ultimately getting locked.

What a reputation for being a cop.

Oh shit,
Turn the music down lets avoid the attention.
They in a bush to the left with a strong intuition...

For D.W.B...

I see the NYPD and probably other state PD's constantly antagonizing
those of no harm.

Having a kid under your arm or chatting with your mom or saying
you're cool and you're calm while your hands are behind your back but
they're twisting your arm has no relevance in approach because you are
already being criminalized like you got caught with a bomb.

Is jail a farm?
Because we're considered animals that need to be tamed,
So the tamer is a farmer/cop that also needs to grow their crop to boost
their name.
Their crop are the number of successful arrest and the most obtain
the fame,
Leading to false accusations, just for the fame, bringing degrade upon
our name.

I'm sorry to the good
To the credible
To the honest that are real.

Those cops have my respect and their bravery will always give me chills.

From experience those are the minority and I doubt I will change how
I feel.

But hey...maybe there's some heroes out there that can show that
they're real.

    –G. Carter

Immune

So in tune
I'm immune
Immune to the tune.

Immune to the tune of the tortured souls tormented by society's voice.

Immune to the tune of society's voice that tortures the mind, by
promoting to buy, promoting the crimes, and promoting the rare
that shine;

Which is ultimately promoting a lie.

So in tune
I'm immune
Immune to the tune.

Immune to the tune of the treacherous targeting all how to live.

You need this
You need that
And in time you'll need this, cuz the that that you have will belongs in
the trash.

So in tune
I'm immune
Immune to the tune.

So I'm in tune with the Sun that provides warmth upon us.
I'm in tune with the Sun which we revolve,
And think is beautiful as it rises and falls.

I'm in tune with waterfalls;
A flowing journey leading to a dropping journey leading to another
journey that flows.

The cycle of life.

So in tune
I'm immune
Immune to the tune.

I'm immune to the noise and in tune with nature.
Nature is the night shining stars.
Nature is the shining sparkling effect the Sun has on water.
Nature is the shhhhh from the trees as the wind glides through
the leaves.
Nature is the conscious thought of when I breathe, I feed the living green
and that reciprocation keeps me alive and at ease.

I'm one with nature that makes me:

So in tune
I'm immune
Immune to the tune.

Immune to the tunes that aren't connected to nature and my internal
happiness and health.

Go explore.

    –G. Carter

Nigger Nigga Mythology

This a heartfelt story.
A young black nigga on the road to the glory.
I say nigga cuz I figure if I heard it at the age of 3 then it must be a part of me.
Come here lil nigga let me give you a dollar.
Come here lil nigga let me fix ya collar.
Watch out my niggas my little nigga is nice.
I hear nigga gimme my money while they rolling the dice.

As I take a blast into the past,
I see why the word nigga is being abused so much.
Picture your limbs from your toes to your noggin being brutally abused with a bat leading to you bound to a crutch.
The bat is the word nigger,
The crutch is our mentality.

Because nigger brought mental fatigue,
Mental fatigue reciprocated with endearment.
Love conquers all, right?
So if you take the word Nig-Ger; which was and is used as barbarity to stereotype and stigmatize Blacks.
And transform it to a word that has similarities to acknowledgement, comrade, friend or brother/sister;
Nigga now becomes a defensive mechanism that says, you can't use the word nigger to mentally abuse me anymore.

And to throw it in your face we're going to use it toward each other repetitively in a good way;

What's good my nigga!

So the mentality turns a negative to a semi positive.

Lots of individuals say people are ignorant for using the word nigga.
They say they obviously don't know their history;
Which I agree with.

A lot of people don't know their history.

At the same time, what about the individuals who do know their history?
I'm no historian but:

I know about the Malcolm's, the King's, NAACP, Black Panthers, Fred
Hampton, Angela Davis, the Harlem Renaissance, Emmitt Til, Ernie
Barnes, the Madam Cj Walkers and the creation of Blues and Jazz.
Which is still mediocre!

The word Nigga has been used in a semi positive context probably from
birth to when media or other perspective told him/her otherwise. And
STILL, it probably was continuously said. Especially if you were born
after the year 1980. So you can't be COMPLETELY upset or disappointed
at those individuals who say it

The point is, Nigga was repetitively used amongst each other that the
word became evolutionary.

Nigga is so popular, other races started using it because they noticed how
much we were using it in a positive way toward each other (sometimes
toward another race) that they feel they can use it to connect to us.

The word expanded even more!

Now Nigga isn't only used by or directed to Blacks anymore.

It is used by other races toward another opposing race as a way to
communicate acknowledgement, comrade, friend or brother/sister.

Which is interesting.

What is the effect of Nigger/Nigga?
So the next question would be, what does a gun do and how does
it sound?
Ch Ch

POW
Fa Ta Da Ba
Boom.
Read it again in slow motion and visualize.
Ch Ch, is the cock of the gun.
POW, is shooting the gun.
Fa Ta Da Ba, is the travel and sound of the bullet.
Boom, is the bullet hitting its target.

Nigger is like a verbal bullet hitting you shot from the wrong host;
In a matter of 3 seconds,
Pandemonium.

Ch Ch becomes thoughts,
POW becomes Nigger verbally said,
Fa Ta Da Ba becomes you hearing the word nigger,
Boom is the effect the word has on you.

That process is slightly altered when someone Black says the word Nigga.
Ch Ch isn't a thought process anymore;
It's instinctual.
Resulting in the Boom effect for Nigga becoming acceptance.

The goal is to get to a point of being bullet proof and not letting the word
Nig-Ger have an effect on you.
That context is used to provoke and degrade Blacks.

But if you have a mindset that knows Blacks have prevailed through
catastrophe and excelled at accomplishing achievements extraordinary
like figuring out the trajectory of a rocket ship to get to the moon; kudos
to Katherine Johnson,

You should have no trouble with laughing in the face of a provoker and walking away.

When old folk here that word they become extremely bothered.
They take that word serious and I don't blame them, because the era they have experienced Nigger was a treacherous thing to say.
Picture living in a society where ya bitched and stripped where ya soul is ripped and balls are snipped and for dessert you're choked then lynched!
Barbarity at its worst.
Old Folk are entitled to their discomfort.
Respect should be shown by making an effort to avoid the word Nigger, or Nigga in their presence.

This is a new era and as I said before Nigga has become evolutionary.
This is a new way of justification for using the word Nigga.
Condoning it or not is on you.

Nigger Nigga Mythology

–G. Carter

To Pops

Yo Pee Oh Pee
Listen up
Buckle up
Hold ya blunt.

This the time I take on a journey so I can open up.
Always contemplated why you left and where you gone,
Was a young boy in streets banging putting on.

Started off in LB, then had my own gang.
DWG Da Worlds Greatest was the name
I had the fame.

Putting cats under me
Viciously.
Doing 30 seconds in the box until uh victory.
If a nigga challenge me,
I brutally finish B,
My hands was something seriously,
Junior High catastrophe.

Being at the top always came with a duty.
Met a lot of false kats that was really tryna fool me,
So I kept the gang tight
We started thinking bout them flights,
I'm talking bout them Nike Flights,
So I had to find a scheme that guaranteed my money right.

(I looked up to you back then. You was the only idol I knew. I use to
constantly think what happened to you.
Sheesh!)

You always on the block on the hustle for the gwap.
I always in the halls pushing selling candy rock.
Everybody knew you,
Everybody knew me,
We was always on the scene in fresh long t.

I wasn't getting booty
But the ladies called me cutie
So I got a couple kisses and I grabbed a couple boobies.

Young girls use to gather up and rate me on a paper.
Got 9s and 10s then I saw uh 8
Who's the hater?

Found out it was Ju,
Remember Ju?
The tall pretty girl,
Long hair with an attitude.

I reminisce about the day you took us to the clinic.
You didn't act manic.
You told me I'm 16 there's no need to panic.
You said you and mom dukes had me at the age of 17 and so could I.

You never gave good advice so I never listen.
I never repent cuz I never wanted children.

That was the first time I felt like you held me down,
Still think about days you came through from outta town… and held
it down.

(That's when you use to come to all my AAU games. I guess that's when I
had a support system, and the reason why I was killing the competition.)

I was doing trickery like I'm David Blane,
Driving to the lane clapping boards cuz my game insane,
AAU is when I had the fame
With the nappy braids,
I averaged 23 points a game
I always used my brain.

The only motivation that I had was you by my side.
You smoked a joint
Pulled me over
And told me we were ride or die.

When we went to games
I looked at your eyes
You were fried.
But you told me that I'm gon kill it and said it with some pride.

Running up and down the court.
Running up and down the court.
Yelling that my boy
While you running up and down the court.

This is my official thanks
For being a father to son it was really great
But times got ruff where mommy had to compensate
Cuz you wasn't there so she had to play the man and the woman
Now imma describe devastate!

Seeing hurt in her eyes,
She stayed strong and never cried.
We were living in a bad spot,

But he's a good guy.
He was always in a tough spot but he did try.
He was on his own cuz his mother up and left
Went to Mississippi so he had to find a place to rest.
Lived from place to place and he couldn't get a job.

I'm giving blank nods,
In my head I'm hearing weak sobs,
Cuz a real father trumps all jobs,
I'm done hearing the sobs nigga!

I needed you when I was riding on the bench!
I had trash games where everyone smelt my stench!
There was times I use to treat women like shit,
I use to hit and run and in my mind I still was the shit.

Cuz of you your girl took my identity
Went months with my name and didn't pay for utilities.
Four thousand dollars in debt ya gotta be kidding me!
Yall dooming yall lives that will last for infinity.

But I'm about forgiveness and letting go.
My true nature as a King is about to show.
So imma speak on your behalf as you really should.

And tell you what I would have told me.

Young G this your pops and I wanna say I'm sorry.
Wish I was the father that had money for a Ferrari.
Contributed on the hardly;
Its cuz I was living in the jungle and didn't want you on that safari.

You was a tough kid but played emotional while on the court.
So I yelled on the side, saying kill em on the court.
Every time that I spoke I can see you went harder;
So I yelled even louder, YOU THE SHIT MR. CARTER!

Boy listen,
When you lived the life that I lived,
There's no turning back so I did what I did.

You my first born and the best move that I made.
I woulda been better if me and mommy was the same,
But I fucked it up and still look at all that you became.

You held it down by sending money when I needed.
You told me to keep my head high and never show when I'm defeated.
I love you my G that's my word that I mean it.

The toughest barriers go to soldiers that can break through.
You pushed through, but remember even warriors can break too.

So live your life like a boss,
Imagine life as a King,
You have a heart of a lion to accomplish anything.

Be great my son...

Pops, despite your absence and neglect I had to face,
I felt like we were cat and mouse and it was me that had to chase.
Not for a kill but for your love; I needed a father in my life.
You're the cat and I'm the mouse chasing fatherly advice.

As time passed resentment almost turned the mouse into a rat
Inside the negative emotion almost led him to a trap
Avoiding hate opened up a catapult into a love
It flung him up so the mouse can use maneuvers from above
From above, the mouse could see sincerity within the cat
The cat wept and wondered how the mouse could easily accept
It wasn't easy but the cat needed something genuine
So the mouse dropped wisdom motivation inspiration
So the cat could imagine cultivation
Which will lead to the cat understanding his final destination
Which is BACK TO HIS SON!

This is me calling out to you
A son to his father
A son seeking serenity
A son seeking love
But if I have to be the father and you be the son
Then son, you are my sun that has given strength and life to me.
And in return, I shall give you something to always be proud of…

Me

    –G. Carter

Yea I used to walk around with my pants sagging. I use to be a bully. I used to fight. I did the gang life. I use to steal a lot. I use to disrespect others on the daily basis and think I was cool for it. Yes I have cheated in my life. Cheated on a test. Cheated on previous girls. Cheated to win a game. Yup, I told lies to my mother, my co-workers, my teachers and my friends before. I'm not perfect.

Yea I enjoy wearing professional attire. I seek to help bullies. I fight for the rights of my people. I steal the floor to facilitate activities at work. I give respect to everyone on a daily basis and feel phenomenal about it. Yes I am a man of integrity. I show that to my lady. To my family. To my co-workers. To my friends. But I'm not perfect.

What's perfect is the fact that I'm not perfect. I get to constantly watch myself grow. The significance in that growth is being conscious that my stumbles won't last forever. So as I live and I learn, I prevail and I progress, and appreciate the life I possess.

You have rode in my maturation rollercoaster and I hope you enjoyed my journey. Reflect upon the pieces that connected with you, and most importantly DO SOMETHING ABOUT IT!

I wish you Peace and Prosperity!

> Thank you,
> Grequan Carter

Acknowledgements

I find it imperative to constantly acknowledge you, mother. You're my savior, my guardian angel, my advisor, my inspiration. You are the best parent anyone in the world can ask for! Thank you for all you have done for me. I'm truly blessed to have such an amazing soul as my mother. I love you. I'm going to continue to strive for greatness and make you proud. I can't wait to see the look on your face when I buy you a car or a house. You deserve to live in royal ambience as a Queen, and with the best of my ability, you will get that experience. You mean the world to me!

I acknowledged my immediate family in my "Ohana" piece. So I wanted to send love and harmony to all of my other relatives. Our encounters are minimum but powerful during engagements. Our DNA connects us, no matter the distance. We are the fruit to our ancestor's labor, so let's be rooted by the appreciation of life, freedom and each other. So to the: **Williams, Carters, Currys, Llyods, Mays, Burtons, Stevens, Scotts** and now **Belchers**, I wish you all Peace and Prosperity.

Acknowledgement must go to all of my former coaches. Each coach has shaped some quality that I still possess today.

Coach Hill, my very first coach. Thank you for changing my form and supporting me through the process. You always had great energy and represented the Black community in a positive light. You're a role model.

Coach Webster, you always had faith in me. You knew my game down to the T and constantly put me in situations of success. I respected you more than any other person during those years. I can finally say, you had a hell of a jump shot. Thank you for having my back.

Coach Larry, I been a Viper since day 1! We killed the AAU and CYO circuit. We have many tournaments under our belts! I will forever cherish those memories. Thank you for never doubting my game and helping me boost my confidence. I even got a coaching championship because of you, thank you. I wish you the best of luck down in Florida. NYC Vipers legacy will live forever because of you.

Rest in Peace **Coach Granby**. He was a legendary Queens New York basketball coach with over 700 wins under his belt. This man CONSTANTLY wanted the best for me. Not being on the right path in high school, he gave me an inestimable amount of guidance trying to get me on a positive track. My disobedience didn't stop his attempts either. I wish he could have seen the man I've became, he would be proud. His guidance shapes and sparks my ambition to help young teens prevail through tough times. He was a great man!

Coach Schoener, you changed my life. You're a genius of a coach. You put me in the best physical shape of my life. You are a great role model that constantly shows respect to others. You have shown me how to be discipline, punctual, and honest. The most important lesson I have learned from you is hard work manifest results. That affected me on and off the court, where my grades started to improve and my overall game. I've learned a lot from you and wish nothing but success for you and your girls. **Coach Rayess** you were a contributing factor to my growth during those 2 years as well, thank you.

Coach Spanbauer, WE GOT A SUNYAC CHAMPIONSHIP! You're a great man on and off of the court. You're a major contributing factor to my leadership mentality. You appointed me the captain of the team where you showed me how to lead by example. You respected my point of views and let me make crucial decisions. My current ability to lead is because of our experiences, thank you! C-State forever!

Other coaches that deserve acknowledgement are **Coach Martin, Coach Ron, Felix, Coach Thomas, RIP Coach Mark, Coach Chuck (Gregg Vance is a legend), Coach Sean, Coach Vickers. Coach Naclerio,** you get acknowledgement because you're a very successful coach and you initially recruited me that first year. When I transferred out that second year I was marked as soft and a quitter. I used those comments as fuel when I became fatigued during work outs to keep me going, so thank you.

Arif, Dj, Khalid, Sean, Joe you already know what it is! The movie life is for an eternity. I will NEVER forget the unique experiences we had. Whether we're distant or close, my loyalty to our friendship will remain intact. We all "glew" up in our own way and to be completely honest, you all are my seeds! I love yall.

I've developed a brotherhood with MANY individuals growing up, playing ball, from schools and in the work place. Each team I played for, there were individuals I connected with more than others but overall every person played a part in my success.

Quay, Ish, Ty, Shak, Loddy, Stef, Hak, Howard, IT, Matt, Marv, Cisco, Diamonte, Mo, Joe, Reef, Dj, Lid, Sean. Delhi was an epic experience, we all did a lot of damage there lol.

Lem, Tj, Golden, Matt, Mike, Prenda, Paul, Ty, T.Felder, Shay-Mart, Blair, Lucky, Kellz, JMO, Carrel, Drew, Dre, Rell, Zay, JP, Coop, Zach, Dan, Jeff, Riv. The Red Dragon brotherhood is forever.

I must acknowledge people I've met along the way, developing good friendships with. **Beatrice, JR, Andre S., Andy/David, Devon L., Josue,**

Rell, Nick-Chin, Aaron J., Nykema, Tyrell R., KJ, White-Mike, Mike/50, Tyrique, Smeak, Mikaela, the Sooks brothers, Darien F., Jazmine, Mo, Lindsey. I'm sure I forgot many, but it's all love. If we formed a bond that's what matters. I appreciate you all!

Mcallan, you are the little brother I always wanted. You're going to accomplish great things in life, I'm sure of it. Keep working on your game and continue to find your path of life. Your mother is amazing and her food is spectacular. Shoot for the stars! And remember, you'll NEVER be able to check me on the court.

My career pursuits and professionalism cannot go with me acknowledging the Recreation, Parks and Leisure Department at the college I graduated from. I've never been exposed to such extravagant, intelligent, pure hearted, beautiful, welcoming group of individuals. You all are the epitome of what professionals should exemplify. I have the upmost respect for you all. **Sharon T., Amy D., Vicki W., Susan W., Susan B., Andrew P., Anderson Y., Darleen L., Esther V.**, I want to thank you from the bottom of my heart for sharing your genius with me and giving purpose to my life. I will do my best to represent our department in the most positive light. Thank you!

I have much love and respect for Caralie F., Michael C., Susan S., Loni W. and everyone affiliated with SportsNet and CP.

Caralie you don't understand how much I appreciate you! You made my internship happen by putting your ALL into meeting requirements, collaborating with CP and making sure I would be able to achieve my goals. You're a phenomenal professional and an amazing CTRS. Your ability to redirect behaviors, help any individual in the world understand a concept, following things by the book and outdoor savviness; has increases by ability to take my own path. Oh yea, I can't forget about your love for people taking pictures of you lol. On the serious note, you have a beautiful soul and you change lives by the day. Thank you from the bottom of my heart.

Mike, you have been a major influence in the professional world and in my personal life. You're a jack of all trades, with a mission to provide recreational opportunities for people of all abilities. You have shown me the ins and outs of management and ways of being successful behind the scenes. Thank you for sharing your wisdom and experiences; I truly needed it. I will forever be grateful for your contributions, you trusting in my abilities and putting me in situations of success. You're going to be a great father. Continue to strive for greatness and I'll see you at the top.

David F., you have been a mentor to me. Showing me, by saying "the sun felt like a hot iron pressed on my skin" is way more effective than saying "it was hot outside." The writing techniques you've taught me only play a mediocre part in why I appreciate you. Your character has revealed a man of good will and compassion. You offered me an open door and gave a males perspective I desperately needed. The constant wisdom you shared will never be forgotten, for it has made me a better man today, and has motivated me to continue to strive for greatness. Thank you!

Justine P., you played a pivotal role in my life. We basically grew up together and experienced lots of "grown up" things. As I reflect, I believe my reality wouldn't be what it is today without your contributions. You helped me bridge the gap, pushing me to think about a future for myself. You've always been an exceptional thinker and an extremely empathetic, compassionate daughter and sister. The act of giving will continue to keep you blessed. One of the most difficult challenges I had to face in life, was coming to terms with how my actions affected your first college experience and overall, affected you. From the most genuine and sincere place within me, I'm truly sorry. You deserve happiness, and I hope you find someone that can manifest that for you. I wish you the best of luck in the medical field and as I told you from the beginning, I hope you're sharing your talent of cosmetology because you are phenomenal at it. Thank you for helping me grow.

Jason Curry, I never expressed this to you before, but you were a major role model to me, from a distance. You're work ethic is phenomenal! You created an empire that has respect all through the United States. Much respect to Big Apple Basketball. Because of you, an inestimable amount of individuals have had the opportunity to get exposure from all levels of colleges and all levels of professional basketball. You helped people develop their skill so they can play at the next level, and have helped multiple players become pros. I can honestly say you're a machine based on the workouts we had together. I respect your hustle and I wish you the best of luck with your pursuits. I miss your mom as well!

Lamar, I wanted to thank you for being a positive male role model for me. You took the time to share your wisdom, enlightening me on finances and how to run a successful business. Not only that, we connected through basketball where our competitive natures constantly collided, leading to battles on big or small rims. I believe I have majority victories lol. On the serious note, you have been a great person to seek guidance from and have led by example on how to be a great father. Your son is bound to greatness. Thank you.

To the **Carter/Kitt family**, **Man**, **G.G.**, **Jaleek**, **Aunt Jennifer**, **Uncle Rob**, **Uncle Shob**, most of our bonding and encounters took place in my childhood. That doesn't diminish the love I will always have for you all. Man, G.G. and Jaleek, growing up with yall made me feel as if I was another brother. That overall experience was very interesting, full of adventure, exploration and competition. From constant play fights to real fights, to walking to Bayswater Park, to stealing snacks from the corner store, to playing football and basketball and overall doing whatever we want, I will always cherish our experiences. Continue to support your individual families and be great fathers! Peace and Prosperity!

Josue & Rell, there was a time I considered you both my best friends. The best of my teen years came from being around you both. We have plenty of great moments together; from me immediately giving Rell buckets the first day I met him to all of us blacking out on Josue's birthday. Our brotherhood was strong and those memories will be with me forever. I'm glad to see yall making money moves, I wish yall nothing but a successful future. Much love.

Jane S. you're a vibrant vibration. A sensational soul. Thank you for expanding my horizon and increasing my consciousness of the many connections in this current life. Your legacy will live forever through your bloodline, your artistic creations, and through the many others you have influenced in a positive way. I'm extremely grateful our paths have crossed!

Deniqua, it is hard to write about you and not want to write something poetic. But then again, our entire story is an endless movie, which is poetic! You have brought so much serenity into my life that I can only rebuttal with offering the purest me. That may be a gift and a curse, because as you know, I play all day. But that's ok! I know you are meant to experience my playfulness and wisdom as I am meant to experience your creativity and intuition. You are my best friend and I am truly blessed that you will be the mother of our son. Thank you for being an extraordinary support system and a phenomenal partner. I Love You!

If you got to this point in the book, MUCH RESPECT! Your support will never go unnoticed. This first project means the world to me and you took the time out to experience what I have to offer. That is truly a blessing! This goes to show you, anything is possible! This is only the beginning! *I HAVE FUTURE PROJECTS ON THE WAY, SO FOLLOW MY INSTAGRAM @* **SKYHIGHIVATION** for release dates. Also, shoot me an email at skyhighivation@gmail.com about your thoughts on the book or specific pieces of interest. For a **LIVE PERFORMANCE** of specific pieces in the book, contact me via email for bookings. Thank you again!

Love is its own entity...

The Ultimate Treasure

23,8,1,20   25,15,21   4,5,19,9,18,5   9,19   23,8,1,20   25,15,21
3,1,14   1,3,17,21,9,18,5

14,15   13,1,20,20,5,18   8,15,23   7,18,1,14,4   15,18
13,9,14,9,1,20,21,18,5

9,20   3,1,14   2,5   25,15,21,18,19

How do you get there?

1,12,12   9,20   20,1,11,5,19   9,19   1   22,9,22,9,4
9,13,1,7,9,14,1,20,9,15,14   1,14,4   3,15,14,19,9,19,20,5,14,3,25

23,8,9,3,8   23,9,12,12   7,18,1,22,9,20,1,20,5   25,15,21,18
4,5,19,9,18,5

15,18   7,18,1,22,9,20,1,20,5   1,14   9,14,20,5,18,14,1,12
21,18,7,5   6,15,18   1,3,20,9,15,14   20,15,23,1,18,4   20,8,1,20
4,5,19,9,18,5

20,8,9,19   19,15,21,18,3,5   15,6   16,15,23,5,18   9,19
21,14,12,9,13,9,20,5,4

2,21,20   25,15,21   13,21,19,20   2,5,12,9,5,22,5!

You're Welcome!
–G. Carter